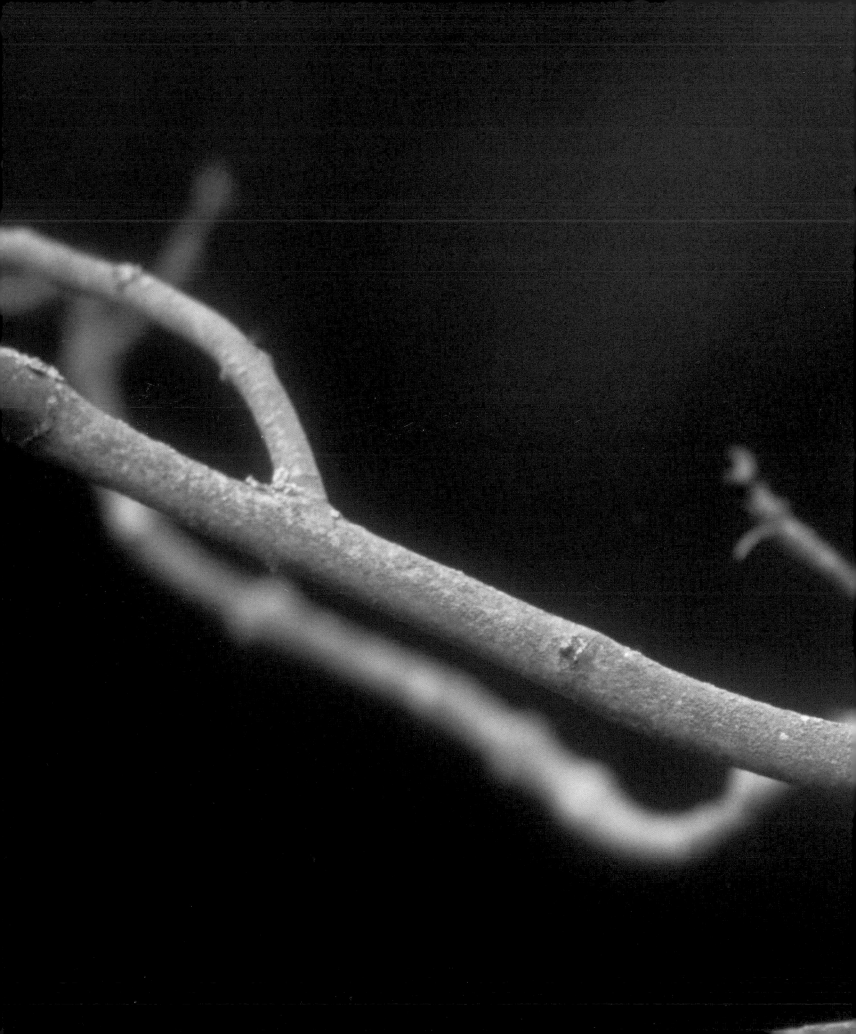

THE WILD WORLD OF ANIMALS

# MONKEYS

MARY HOFF

CREATIVE EDUCATION

*Special thanks to Dr. Sue Boinski, University of Florida.*

Published by Creative Education, 123 South Broad Street, Mankato, Minnesota 56001. Creative Education is an imprint of The Creative Company. Designed by Rita Marshall. Production design by The Design Lab. Photographs by Alamy (Michael J. Kronmal), Corbis (Bettmann, Tom Brakefield, Michael & Patricia Fogden, Hulton–Deutsch Collection, Wolfgang Kaehler, Renee Lynn, Buddy Mays, David A. Northcott, Douglas Peebles, Kevin Schafer, Stuart Westmorland), Getty Images (Fox Photos, National Geographic), kevinschafer.com, Roy Toft. Copyright © 2006 Creative Education. International copyright reserved in all countries. No part of this book may be reproduced in any form without written permission from the publisher. Printed in the United States of America. Library of Congress Cataloging-in-Publication Data: Hoff, Mary King. Monkeys / by Mary Hoff. p. cm. — (The wild world of animals). ISBN 1-58341-352-9. 1. Squirrel monkeys—Juvenile literature. I. Title. II. Wild world of animals (Creative Education). QL737.P925H64 2004. 599.8—dc22. 2004056161. First edition 9 8 7 6 5 4 3 2 1

It's a sunny morning in the rain forest of Surinam, a country in northern South America. The sounds of birds calling and singing fill the air. High above the ground, dozens of tiny monkeys are climbing around in a **cecropia** tree. Young ones play among the branches. Adults search through the leaves for fruit and insects to eat. Suddenly, a shadow appears. A hawk is flying over the forest in search of a monkey meal. Some of the monkeys call out an alarm. They scurry to safer perches where they can avoid the hawk's sharp claws.

Hawks can spot monkeys from high above the trees **5**

## SMALL WONDERS

Monkeys are **mammals** with long arms and legs. Most monkeys live in the **tropics**. There are many kinds of monkeys, from the pocket-sized pygmy marmoset of South America to the huge, blue-faced mandrill of Africa. Those that live in Africa or Asia are called Old World monkeys. Those that live in South America or Central America are called New World monkeys. One well-known kind of New World monkey is the squirrel monkey.

Squirrel monkeys (opposite) and a hamadryas baboon (left)   **7**

Squirrel monkeys are smaller than most other monkeys. They weigh about 20 to 40 ounces (567–1,134 g). Their bodies are about 12 inches (30 cm) long. Males are bigger than females.

When you see a squirrel monkey, one of the first things you notice is its long tail. A squirrel monkey's tail can be 16 inches (40 cm) long—longer than its body!

Another thing that stands out about a squirrel monkey is its color. The hair on much of a squirrel monkey's body is reddish, black, or gray. Its arms, legs, and back are yellow. The tip of its tail and the skin on its face are black. It has white, hairy ears.

Squirrel monkeys have short, soft, thick fur

Like most kinds of monkeys, squirrel monkeys live in trees. Many live in dense rain forests. Others live in **mangrove swamps**. Squirrel monkeys like to be near water. Other animals that live in areas where squirrel monkeys live include capuchin monkeys, bats, jaguars, bees, beetles, hummingbirds, and parrots.

Monkeys have many **adaptations** that help them live high in the trees. Their eyes are in the front of their head, rather than on the sides as is the case for many other animals. This means that monkeys can look at things with both eyes at the same time, which helps them tell how far away something is.

Macaws (opposite) and beetles (left) live high in the trees, too **11**

Long arms and legs help monkeys climb around in trees. Squirrel monkeys' **dexterous** hands and feet allow them to grasp skinny branches. Short upper leg bones and long lower leg bones give squirrel monkeys lots of power for jumping from one tree limb to another. A squirrel monkey can jump a distance of up to eight feet (2.4 m)!

Monkeys jump to high or low branches to find food **13**

Monkeys' tails are important for life in the trees, too. Unlike some other New World monkeys, a squirrel monkey cannot hang by its tail. But the tail helps it keep its balance as it climbs through the tree limbs—much as a long pole helps a tight-rope walker balance.

**14**    Squirrel monkeys rarely come down from trees

## LIFE AS A MONKEY

If you like crowds, you might like being

a monkey. Like other monkeys, squirrel

monkeys live in groups. Each group may

contain from a dozen to several hundred

individuals. The mothers and their babies

hang out together. The males gather in

another area.

Monkeys are surrounded by thousands of rain forest plants

Most monkeys are diurnal, or active during the day. Squirrel monkeys sleep close to each other at night. In the morning, the monkeys go off to **forage**. At the end of the day, they come back together. Sometimes they sleep with other kinds of monkeys. When resting, a squirrel monkey may curl its tail over its shoulder.

Squirrel monkeys are very active. Young monkeys play with each other, wrestling or pretending to fight. The adults groom each other, combing through one another's fur to pick out dirt and insects. Monkeys can be noisy, too. Scientists have found that squirrel monkeys make more than two dozen different sounds, including whistles, chirps, and trills. Each sound has its own meaning. Squirrel monkeys also communicate with each other through actions and odor.

Monkeys enjoy being near each other    **19**

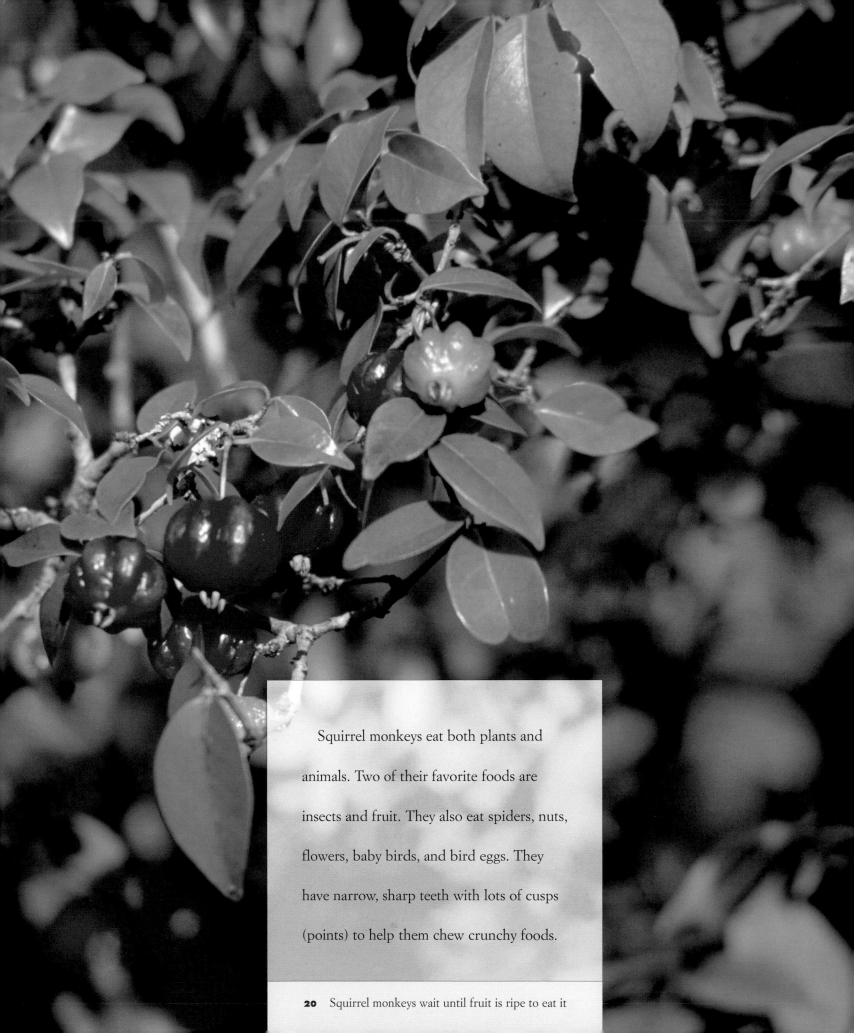

Squirrel monkeys eat both plants and animals. Two of their favorite foods are insects and fruit. They also eat spiders, nuts, flowers, baby birds, and bird eggs. They have narrow, sharp teeth with lots of cusps (points) to help them chew crunchy foods.

Squirrel monkeys wait until fruit is ripe to eat it

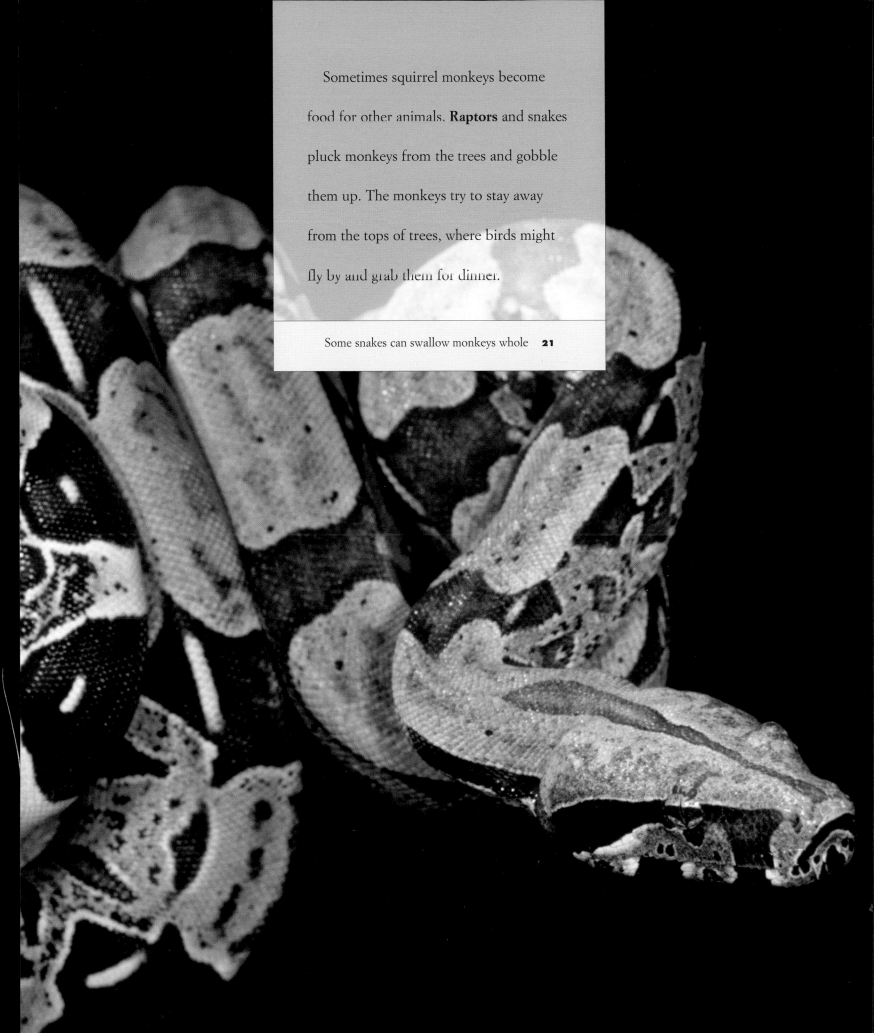

Sometimes squirrel monkeys become food for other animals. **Raptors** and snakes pluck monkeys from the trees and gobble them up. The monkeys try to stay away from the tops of trees, where birds might fly by and grab them for dinner.

Some snakes can swallow monkeys whole **21**

Male squirrel monkeys gain weight before mating season, making them look bigger and stronger. Females gain weight, too, as their bodies prepare to feed a baby. Five to six months after mating, the young are born. As with most other monkeys, squirrel monkeys give birth to a single infant.

Squirrel monkeys can climb almost as soon as they are born. But they spend much of their time clinging to their

Squirrel monkeys eat a lot before mating season

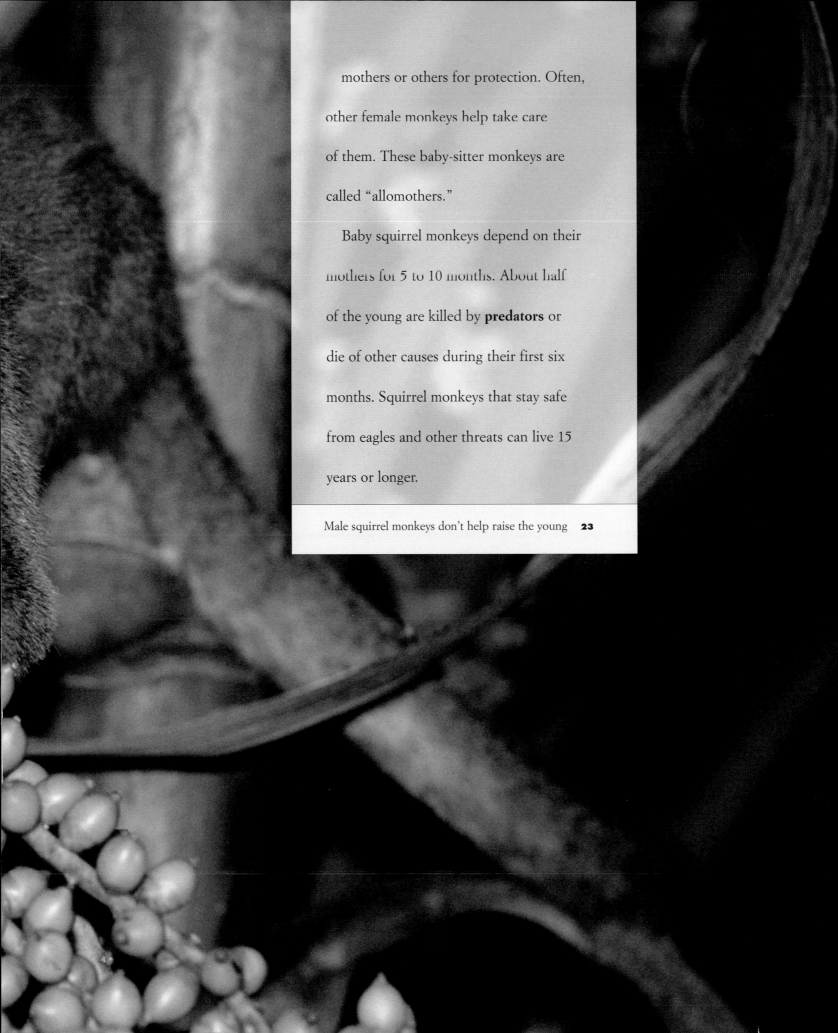

mothers or others for protection. Often, other female monkeys help take care of them. These baby-sitter monkeys are called "allomothers."

Baby squirrel monkeys depend on their mothers for 5 to 10 months. About half of the young are killed by **predators** or die of other causes during their first six months. Squirrel monkeys that stay safe from eagles and other threats can live 15 years or longer.

Male squirrel monkeys don't help raise the young **23**

## HUMAN CONNECTIONS

People who live near monkeys sometimes capture them for food, just as people who live in other places hunt and eat wild rabbits and deer. Farmers who grow fruit sometimes kill squirrel monkeys to protect their crops from being eaten.

**24** A sailor feeds a monkey on board a ship, 1929

People who don't live near monkeys in the wild have contact with them, too. Squirrel monkeys are very popular pets because they are small and cute. Monkeys also have been captured for zoos. Many monkeys, including squirrel monkeys, have been used in scientific experiments to learn about human health and illnesses.

Pet monkeys need a lot of care and attention    **25**

A monkey named Gordo was probably the world's most famous squirrel monkey. He became a hero in 1959 when scientists sent him into space in a rocket. They wanted to see how the conditions of outer space would affect people. Gordo was the first monkey in space and helped show that people can survive space travel. Other monkeys have flown in space since then.

Monkeys wear special equipment when they go into space   **27**

Today, monkeys around the world are having a harder and harder time finding places to live because people are destroying their **habitat**. People are cutting down trees to build businesses. They are also replacing rain forests with farmland. Some squirrel monkeys are killed by chemicals that farmers use to keep their crops from being eaten by insects.

**28** Monkeys need trees for food and shelter

The number of squirrel monkeys in the world is decreasing. In some places, there are so few squirrel monkeys that people fear they could disappear completely. One type of squirrel monkey is on the endangered species list, which keeps track of animals that could become **extinct**.

Many people are working to help monkeys of all kinds thrive. Some are preserving rain forests as wild areas for monkeys. Others are working to prevent illegal hunting. Still others are teaching people about monkeys so that they will appreciate and care for them. If enough people care about monkeys and do their share to protect the habitat in which they live, these fascinating creatures will remain a healthy part of our wild world.

Some monkeys are very affectionate **31**

## GLOSSARY

**Adaptations** are things about a plant or animal that help it survive where it lives.

**Cecropia** is a short, umbrella-shaped tree that grows in rain forests.

When a creature is **dexterous**, it works well with its hands or paws.

An animal that is **extinct** can no longer be found alive anywhere on Earth.

To **forage** is to search for the food needed to live and grow.

The place where a creature lives is called its **habitat**.

**Mammals** are animals that depend on milk for food when they are young.

**Mangrove swamps** are forests that contain mangroves, trees that grow in standing water.

**Predators** are animals that kill and eat other animals.

**Raptors** are birds such as hawks, eagles, and owls that capture and eat other animals.

The part of the world near the equator is known as the **tropics**.

## BOOKS

Grassy, John. *Apes and Monkeys*. Chicago: Kidsbooks, 1997.

Martin, Patricia A. Fink. *Monkeys of Central and South America*. New York: Children's Press, 2000.

Patton, Don. *New World Monkeys*. Plymouth, Minn.: The Child's World, 1996.

## WEB SITES

**Animal Bytes: Monkey** http://www.sandiegozoo.org/animalbytes/t-monkey.html

**Mindy's Memory: Squirrel Monkey Facts** http://www.mindysmem.org/squirrel.html

**Squirrel Monkeys** http://www.squirrel-monkeys.com

## INDEX